TIMELINE

SCIENCE

DINOSAURS

Silver Dolphin

Silver Dolphin Books
An imprint of Printers Row Publishing Group
A division of Readerlink Distribution Services, LLC
10350 Barnes Canyon Road, Suite 100, San Diego, CA 92121
www.silverdolphinbooks.com

ISBN: 978-1-62686-945-5

Manufactured, printed, and assembled in China.
21 20 19 18 17 1 2 3 4 5

Written by Courtney Acampora
Designed by Dynamo Limited

Image Credits:
Images copyright Thinkstock, Superstock, Inc., Judith River Foundation, MCDinosaurhunter, The Lord of the Allosaurs, Nobu Tamura, Parent Géry, NPS, Nils Knötschke, Library of Congress, Prints & Photographs Division, OnFirstWhoIs, Connie Ma, Kabacchi, Paul Hudson, Wellcome Images, Franco Tempesta, John Francis.

CONTENTS

WHERE ON EARTH?

Ankylosaurus

Corythosaurus

Pachycephalosaurus

Tyrannosaurus Rex

North America

Allosaurus

Utahraptor

Brachiosaurus

Maiasaura

Stegosaurus

Coelophysis

Eoraptor

Amargasaurus

South America

The seven continents on Earth were once all connected in one giant landmass called Pangaea. This map, illustrating the continents as they are today, shows where different dinosaur species were discovered. Find out more fascinating facts about each dinosaur inside this book!

Plateosaurus

Avivimus

Archaeopteryx

Europe

Asia

Iguanodon

Velociraptor

Spinosaurus

Africa

Australia

WHAT ARE DINOSAURS?

Imagine a world where large, often ferocious, creatures roamed the land, soared through the air, and swam beneath the seas. That's what Earth looked like around 230 million years ago. Although the word dinosaur makes people think of gigantic prehistoric creatures with weapons for body parts, not all dinosaurs were large or deadly.

For 165 million years, dinosaurs continued to stomp, soar, and swim on Earth, growing in size and in number. But they weren't the only prehistoric creatures. Life on Earth began over 3.6 billion years ago in the oceans and eventually made its way onto land. Plants, bugs, and reptiles were already on Earth by the time dinosaurs arrived.

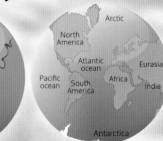

Pangaea
270 million years ago

Laurasia and Gondwana
200 million years ago

Modern World

Before humans inhabited Earth, the planet was much different than it is today. Of course, there were no buildings or roads, and scientists believe that all the land on the planet was crunched together into one big supercontinent called Pangaea. When dinosaurs first emerged, around 230 million years ago, the land was hot and dry. There would have been deserts in some areas, and swamps in others, but no ice and snow except at the Poles.

165 million years later, the planet was getting wetter and cooler, and Pangaea had broken up into the northern supercontinent of Laurasia and the southern supercontinent of Gondwana, later creating the landmasses and bodies of water we know today. And the dinosaurs would only roam this changing Earth for a short time longer.

WHAT DID DINOSAURS LOOK LIKE?

Scientists are able to piece together dinosaur skeletons based on the information they get from fossil impressions and bones. But how do they know what color dinosaurs were?

Ornitholestes

Microraptor

While figuring out how to tell the color of a dinosaur's feathers, scientists found that feathers have melanin, which are pigments, or colors, that are shaped and arranged differently depending on the color. These pigments have survived fossilization, but have changed. Some scientists think the changes melanin goes through over millions of years of fossilization make information about a dinosaur's color inaccurate. Scientists have hypothesized that dinosaurs were gray or green so they were camouflaged in their surroundings. Other scientists think that dinosaurs were bright red, blue, and green to make them stand out and attract a mate! The search goes on...

FUN FACTS

Some dinosaurs had what looked like whiskers. These "whiskers" turned out to be an early development of feathers called protofeathers.

A duck-billed dinosaur named Leonardo is said to be one of the best-preserved dinosaurs found so far. Impressions of its skin and digestive system can be easily seen. Scientists could even tell that this dinosaur's last meal included pine needles!

Leonardo!

Some people think that because many modern birds are colorful and they are descendents of dinosaurs, that dinosaurs may have been colorful too.

Protofeathers and feathers have been found trapped in amber, a fossilized materials from trees, with their colors preserved.

AGE OF THE DINOSAURS

Dinosaurs lived during the Mesozoic era, which is divided into three periods: Triassic, Jurassic, and Cretaceous. The Triassic was 252–201 million years ago, the Jurassic was 201–145 million years ago, and the Cretaceous was 145–66 million years ago.

TRIASSIC

At the beginning of the Triassic period, all of the continents we know today were connected as one supercontinent called Pangaea. Toward the end of the Triassic period, small to medium sized dinosaurs emerged. The world was warm and dry, and Pangaea was beginning to split apart.

JURASSIC

During the Jurassic period, Earth was warm and wet, and the land was covered in trees, ferns, and other greenery. The biggest and most recognizable dinosaurs, including the sauropods, lived during this period.

CRETACEOUS

Dinosaurs continued to thrive and new dinosaurs were coming into being during the Cretaceous period. Paleontologists have found fossils for the first true birds, modern mammal groups, and flowering plants from this time period. Pangaea continued to break apart and the extinction of the dinosaurs occurred.

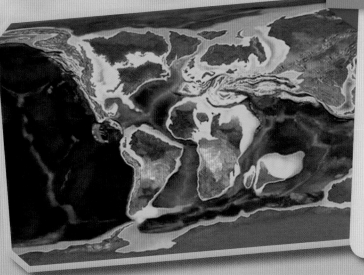

PALEOZOIC		MESOZOIC ERA		CENOZOIC	
	TRIASSIC	JURASSIC	CRETACEOUS		
300	250	200	150	100	50	present

millions of years

DINOSAUR GROUPS

Millions of years ago, hundreds of different types of dinosaurs lived on Earth. In order to make sense of all these different types of dinosaurs, scientists sorted them into two groups, Saurischia and Ornithischia, which are each made up of smaller groups.

SAURISCHIA

Dinosaurs in the Saurischia group are nicknamed "lizard hips" because their pubic bone points towards the front of the animal. Features of the first saurischians include a long neck, grasping hands, and uneven fingers. The Saurischia group includes theropods, like *Tyrannosaurus rex*, and sauropods, like *Brachiosaurus*.

Sauropod

Theropod

Theropods

- "Theropod" means "beast-footed."
- Mostly made up of meat-eating dinosaurs that walked on two legs.
- Notable features: hollow bones, clawed hands, sharp backward-curved teeth, and large eyes.
- Theropods are the only dinosaurs that still exist—they're alive in the form of birds!

Sauropods

- "Sauropod" means "lizard-footed."
- Notable features: small heads and long necks compared to the rest of their bodies.
- Their long necks allowed them to graze without needing to move around much to search for food.
- Small heads didn't leave much room for big brains so sauropods aren't considered to be the most intelligent dinosaurs.

ORNITHISCHIA

Dinosaurs that fall into the Ornithischia group are nicknamed "bird hips." They had hips that looked like a bird's, with all the lower hip bones pointing backward. The Ornithischia group is made up of ornithopods, stegosaurs, pachycephalosaurs, ankylosaurs, and ceratopsians.

Ankylosaur

Pachycephalosauria
- Plant-eaters
- Means "thick-headed, lizard"

Ceratopsia
- Plant-eaters
- Includes horned dinosaurs
- Means "horned face"

Ornithopods
- "Ornithopod" means bird-footed.
- Plant-eaters with beaks that they used for cutting, and teeth used for chewing.
- Lived in herds.

Ankylosauria
- Means "fused lizard"
- Plant-eaters
- Armored; covered in spikes and plates.

Stegosaurs
- Stegosaur means "roof lizard."
- Rows of bony plates ran down their backs and spikes were located on their tails.
- Their teeth were smaller than humans' teeth.

PREHISTORIC CREATURES IN THE AIR AND IN THE SEA

In order for a prehistoric creature to be called a "dinosaur," it needed to live on land. However, other prehistoric creatures were living at the same time as the dinosaurs, in the air and in the sea.

IN THE AIR

Pteranodon lived 85 million years ago and was a small bird–like creature that only weighed about 30 pounds. It had a long beak that was probably used for scooping fish out of the water.

Dorygnathus

Dorygnathus lived 190 million years ago and was even smaller than *Pteranodon*—weighing only 12 pounds. It had a long tail and dagger–like teeth, and could snap up fish from the water.

IN THE SEA

Mosasaurus was a fearsome hunter that lived in the sea 70 million years ago. It was around 50 feet long and weighed 15 tons! With two rows of sharp teeth and a hinged jaw, *Mosasaurus* could swallow food whole.

Mosasaurus

Elasmosaurus also lived in the sea 70 million years ago. *Elasmosaurus* was 45 feet long and weighed three tons. It had a wide body, four big flippers, and a very long neck. It used its overlapping teeth to capture prey, and then swallowed its meal whole.

Dakosaurus lived 150 million years ago and was 15 feet long and weighed two tons. It had a head like a dinosaur and a body that looked like a crocodile.

TRIASSIC DINOSAURS

By the start of the Triassic period, new species of plants and animals were beginning to find their place on Earth.

Eoraptor

Name meaning: Dawn stealer
Size: 3 feet tall; 440 pounds
Diet: Animals
Fossils found: Argentina

Eoraptor was a small, speedy dinosaur that lived in what is now present—day Argentina. Its name means "dawn stealer" because it lived during the dawn, or beginning, of the Age of Dinosaurs. In 1991, an *Eoraptor* was discovered in Argentina's Valley of the Moon by paleontologists Fernando Novas and Paul Sereno.

HERRERASAURUS

Herrerasaurus fossils were discovered in the same place as Eoraptor—Argentina's Valley of the Moon. The first incomplete skeleton was uncovered in 1958 by a farmer named Victorino Herrera, whom the dinosaur is named after. In 1988, paleontologist Paul Sereno discovered a complete skull. Paired with Victorino Herrera's findings, scientists successfully reconstructed the Herrerasaurus.

The lower jaw contained sharp teeth that curved inward that helped Herrerasaurus grip prey.

Herrerasaurus was bipedal, meaning it got around on two legs. Its strong legs allowed the dinosaur to run quickly.

Three curved claws helped Herrerasaurus grasp and rake.

Herrerasaurus

Name meaning: Herrera's Lizard
Size: 13 feet; 463 pounds
Diet: Animals
Fossils found: Argentina

PALEOZOIC	MESOZOIC ERA			CENOZOIC
	TRIASSIC	JURASSIC	CRETACEOUS	

| 300 | 250 | 200 | 150 | 100 | 50 | present |

HERRERASAURUS

EORAPTOR

millions of years

TRIASSIC DINOSAURS

Plateosaurus evolved in the late Triassic period. The discovery of fossils in Germany suggests that they lived in herds.

Plateosaurus

Name meaning: Flat lizard
Size: 23 feet long; 880 pounds
Diet: Plants
Fossils found: Germany, France, Switzerland

A long neck allowed Plateosaurus to reach vegetation high above the ground.

Plateosaurus's hands had four fingers with claws that helped them grasp things, and may have been used for defense.

Its eyes were located high up on the head for a better view of its surroundings.

Coelophysis was a meat-eating dinosaur that belonged to a group of dinosaurs called theropods. Its long, narrow jaw was filled with razor-sharp teeth.

Tough skin may have been covered with protective scales, but it is possible Coelophysis was covered in feathers on top of its head and back.

Coelophysis

Name meaning: Hollow form
Size: 9 feet long; 60 pounds
Diet: Animals
Fossils found: North America

Its mouth was filled with over 50 teeth with saw-like edges.

Strong legs supported its body, as it walked on its hind legs.

Similar to a modern-day chicken, the Coelophysis was one of the earliest dinosaurs that had a wishbone.

Its tail helped Plateosaurus balance when it walked on its back legs.

PALEOZOIC	MESOZOIC ERA			CENOZOIC
	TRIASSIC	JURASSIC	CRETACEOUS	
300	250	200	150	100	50	present

COELOPHYSIS

PLATEOSAURUS

millions of years

JURASSIC DINOSAURS

DIPLODOCUS

Diplodocus lived in western North America and fossils have been found in Wyoming, Montana, and Colorado in the fossil-rich area called the Morrison Formation. It is the most displayed dinosaur in museums because wealthy businessman Andrew Carnegie sold many casts of the fossils in the nineteenth century.

Diplodocus
Name meaning: Double beam
Size: 85 feet long; 44,000 pounds
Diet: Plants
Fossils found: North America

Front teeth were blunt and peg-like and helped comb leaves off of sticks and branches like the tines of a rake.

A long tail could be whipped around quickly to knock down predators.

Its long neck and tail made up most of its total length. Fifteen vertebrae supported the neck.

A layer of tough scales covered its body to protect it from predators.

APATOSAURUS

Apatosaurus was a sauropod that was first described by paleontologist Othniel Charles Marsh in 1877. For many years it was known by the name Brontosaurus, but scientists finally realized that these were two very different dinosaurs.

Apatosaurus

Name meaning: Deceptive lizard
Size: 69 feet long
Diet: Plants
Fossils found: North America

Paleontologists rarely find Apatosaurus skulls because they were thin and could be easily crushed.

Peg-like teeth were used to rake leaves from sticks and branches.

Its long neck allowed Apatosaurus to reach high up in the treetops for food.

Strong, long tail could be used to knock down predators.

PALEOZOIC		MESOZOIC ERA		CENOZOIC
	TRIASSIC	JURASSIC	CRETACEOUS	
300	250	200	150	100	50	present

APATOSAURUS   DIPLODOCUS

millions of years

JURASSIC DINOSAURS

BRACHIOSAURUS

The largest dinosaurs to roam the Earth didn't eat other animals—they ate plants! *Brachiosaurus* had to eat more than 400 pounds of food every day just to survive.

Brachiosaurus
Name meaning: Arm lizard
Size: 85 feet long; 150,000 pounds
Diet: Plants
Fossils found: North America, Africa, Europe

A long neck allowed Brachiosaurus to eat leaves that other dinosaurs could not reach.

Brachiosaurus did not chew its food. Its jaw collected food and the tongue pushed it down.

Brachiosaurus's name means "arm lizard," referring to the length of its front legs, which were longer than its back legs.

ALLOSAURUS

Allosaurus's name means "different lizard." It got this name because its neck bones looked different from the neck bones of other dinosaurs. Allosaurus may have only been half the size of T.rex, but this spine–chilling dino was powerful.

Allosaurus may have had small horns above its eye sockets.

Allosaurus could open its jaw extremely wide. It may have used its top teeth to slice through prey.

Allosaurus
Name meaning: Different lizard
Size: 39 feet long; 4,000 pounds
Diet: Large and small animals
Fossils found: Europe, North America

Each foot contained three toes and one smaller toe on the inside of the foot.

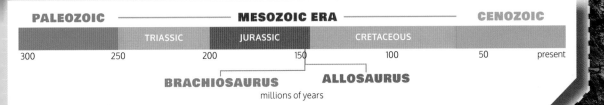

PALEOZOIC		MESOZOIC ERA			CENOZOIC
	TRIASSIC	JURASSIC	CRETACEOUS		
300	250	200	150	100	50	present

BRACHIOSAURUS   ALLOSAURUS

millions of years

JURASSIC DINOSAURS

STEGOSAURUS

Stegosaurus was as big as two rhinoceroses and had tough skin, a heavy, spiked tail, and a brain the size of a golf ball. It would have been a prime target for the hungry meat-eaters of the day. The line of bony plates that stood up along *Stegosaurus*'s back may have helped control its temperature.

Stegosaurus

Name meaning: Roofed lizard
Size: 30 feet long; 6,000 pounds
Diet: Plants
Fossils found: North America

Stegosaurus's back was covered with plates made from bony material. The plates stood up to two feet tall and may have been used for protection, mating and defense, or temperature control.

A flexible tail covered in spikes could be whipped to ward off predators.

Shorter front legs caused Stegosaurus's head to be low to the ground, so it grazed on short plants such as cycads and conifers.

Stegosaurus could not outrun other dinosaurs. It was a slow walker, only slightly faster than a walking human.

ARCHAEOPTERYX

Discovered in 1861, *Archaeopteryx* was a small dinosaur with feathers and wings. Scientists believe it may have been able to fly, though only short distances. So far, only twelve *Archaeopteryx* fossils have been found.

Sharp, pointed teeth helped it catch small animals.

Its second toe had an extremely sharp claw used for killing.

Archaeopteryx had short wings with a sharp claw.

Archaeopteryx

Name meaning: Ancient wing
Size: 18 inches tall; 4 pounds
Diet: Animals
Fossils found: Germany

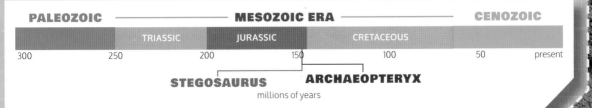

PALEOZOIC		MESOZOIC ERA		CENOZOIC
	TRIASSIC	JURASSIC	CRETACEOUS	
300	250	200	150	100	50	present

STEGOSAURUS   ARCHAEOPTERYX

millions of years

Amargasaurus

Name meaning: Amarga lizard

Size: 35 feet long; 14,000 pounds

Diet: Plants

Fossils found: Argentina

AMARGASAURUS

One of the smaller of the sauropod plant-eaters, *Amargasaurus* was about the size of two elephants. Its fossils were found in a rocky outcrop called La Amarga in Argentina, and revealed that this odd-looking creature probably found its food closer to the ground. The sharp spines on its tail and neck may have held a web-like "sail" of skin across the top of its back, making the animal look bigger than it really was, and possibly helping control its body temperature.

Amargasaurus had sharp spines that made up a sail running along its back. The sail may have changed colors, becoming brighter during mating season.

Its front legs were shorter than its back legs, causing it to lean forward as it walked.

UTAHRAPTOR

Utahraptor was a ferocious dinosaur. These predators had a unique sharp claw on its second toe, used for slashing and stabbing prey. *Utahraptor's* fossilized remains were discovered in 1993 in central Utah.

Utahraptor

Name meaning: Utah thief
Size: 20 feet long; 2,200 pounds
Diet: Animals
Fossils found: North America

Its long snout suggests that *Utahraptor* had an excellent sense of smell that helped it detect prey.

Utahraptor's long foot claw was 9 inches long and used for slicing through prey.

Utahraptor's sharp claws were used for grabbing prey or defense.

Utahraptor was covered in feathers.

PALEOZOIC		MESOZOIC ERA			CENOZOIC	
		TRIASSIC	JURASSIC	CRETACEOUS		
300	250	200	150	100	50	present

AMARGASAURUS

UTAHRAPTOR

millions of years

CRETACEOUS DINOSAURS

IGUANODON

An *Iguanodon* fossil was one of the first fossils ever to be recognized as belonging to a dinosaur. The creature earned its name from its teeth, which look like those of modern iguanas. At twice the weight of an elephant, *Iguanodon* was a big, bulky plant-eater. On the thumbs of its short forearms were scary-looking spikes.

Iguanodon

Name meaning: Iguana tooth
Size: 35 feet long; 12,000 pounds
Diet: Plants
Fossils found: England, Belgium, Spain

Iguanodon had a beaklike mouth that was ideal for eating plants.

A long, stiff tail helped it balance when standing on two legs.

Iguanodon used its padded, webbed hands to walk on ground.

Iguanodon walked on both two and four legs.

ARGENTINOSAURUS

A long neck helped Argentinosaurus reach leaves high up in trees.

One of the biggest dinosaurs to ever walk the Earth, *Argentinosaurus* weighed as much as 13 elephants, and measured 120 feet long. *Argentinosaurus* had a small head and long neck, which helped it reach deep into the trees for food. *Argentinosaurus* swallowed clumps of leaves whole, grinding them up in its stomach. Its feet were wide and round, with short, stubby toes.

Tough scales protected the dinosaur.

Argentinosaurus

Name meaning: Lizard of Argentina
Size: 120 feet long; 200,000 pounds
Diet: Plants
Fossils found: Argentina

Thick, stumpy legs supported its enormous body.

PALEOZOIC		MESOZOIC ERA			CENOZOIC
	TRIASSIC		JURASSIC	CRETACEOUS	
300	250	200	150	100	50	present

IGUANODON

ARGENTINOSAURUS

millions of years

CRETACEOUS DINOSAURS

SPINOSAURUS

Longer than *T.rex*, but living millions of years earlier, *Spinosaurus* was one of the biggest meat-eaters that ever lived. It was most likely a great hunter, and its long, thin snout would have been great for catching fish and tearing into dead animals.

Spinosaurus

Name meaning: Spiny lizard
Size: 46 feet long; 6,000 pounds
Diet: Large and small animals
Fossils found: Africa

The long, spiked sail running along its back stood up to 6 feet tall.

Spinosaurus's snout was similar to that of a crocodile, with nostrils on top so that it could breathe while submerged in water.

Flat, webbed back feet helped Spinosaurus paddle through the water.

Spinosaurus's clawed hands were used for defense.

Sharp, tilted teeth helped Spinosaurus scoop up fish from water.

VELOCIRAPTOR

Velociraptor was a fierce, fast-moving meat-eater about the size of a big turkey. It was an aggressive hunter, had needle-sharp teeth, a long, pointed jaw, and sharp claws on its hands.

Velociraptor

Name meaning: Fast thief
Size: 6 feet long; 35 pounds
Diet: Small animals
Fossils found: China, Mongolia

Velociraptor had excellent vision like most modern birds. The bones of its eyes suggest it may have hunted at night.

Standing upright on two legs, *Velociraptor* adults could run up to 24 miles per hour.

Small forearms made it impossible for *Velociraptor* to fly, even though it shared many characteristics with modern birds.

Velociraptor used 4-inch-long retractable claws on its feet to attack prey.

PALEOZOIC		MESOZOIC ERA			CENOZOIC
	TRIASSIC	JURASSIC	CRETACEOUS		
300	250	200	150	100	50	present

SPINOSAURUS

millions of years

VELOCIRAPTOR

31

CRETACEOUS DINOSAURS

PARASAUROLOPHUS

One of the most unique dinosaurs, *Parasaurolophus* was a crested, duck-billed dinosaur. In fact, its name means "near crested lizard." *Parasaurolophus's* most recognizable feature, its crest, acted like a horn to make loud, bellowing calls used to communicate. Like other duck-billed dinosaurs, *Parasaurolophus* may have traveled in herds.

Its sharp beak was used to snip off leaves.

It used its crest to make loud noises that were used to communicate, find a mate, or warn other *Parasaurolophuses* of danger.

Its thick and heavy tail helped *Parasaurolophus* balance.

Strong, sturdy arms supported *Parasaurolophus* while it browsed for food on all fours.

Parasaurolophus

Name meaning:
Near crested lizard
Size: 36 feet long; 7,700 pounds
Diet: Plants
Fossils found: North America

MAIASAURA

We know a lot about *Maiasaura* because 75 million years ago, a whole herd was killed at the same time and buried in volcanic ash. The result was a treasure trove of fossils for scientists, who have studied *Maiasaura* young and old. They even found eggs with fossils of baby *Maiasaura* still inside. From all the fossils available to them, scientists have determined that this dinosaur took good care of its young. That's how this dinosaur earned its name — "good mother lizard."

Maiasaura

Name meaning: Good mother lizard
Size: 30 feet long; 8,000 pounds
Diet: Plants
Fossils found: North America

Maiasaura was a social dinosaur that nested in groups. It also migrated in groups to search for food.

Maiasaura's toothless beak was used for cutting through plants. Its mouth contained hundreds of teeth for shredding plants.

The number of toes on *Maiasaura*'s front and back feet differed. The hind feet had three toes, whereas the front feet had four.

Maiasaura walked on its hind feet with its tail held out for balance.

PALEOZOIC		MESOZOIC ERA			CENOZOIC	
		TRIASSIC	JURASSIC	CRETACEOUS		
300	250	200	150	100	50	present

PARASAUROLOPHUS   MAIASAURA

millions of years

CRETACEOUS DINOSAURS

AVIVIMUS

Avivimus was a small meat-eating dinosaur that lived in the late Cretaceous period. With its long neck and legs, it looked a bit like a miniature ostrich, but like *Velociraptor*, it was only about the size of a big turkey. *Avivimus* was covered in feathers, but did not fly.

Avivimus

Name meaning: Bird mimic
Size: 5 feet long; 35 pounds
Diet: Small animals and possibly insects
Fossils found: China, Mongolia

Avivimus had short arms that were able to fold like modern birds' wings. Each arm had three sharp claws on the ends.

Avivimus most likely had a large brain for its size.

Long, slender legs helped *Avivimus* quickly chase prey.

Avivimus's toothless beak means it was probably an omnivore that ate nuts, fruit, and small animals.

ANKYLOSAURUS

Ankylosaurus
Name meaning: Fused lizard
Size: 35 feet long; 8,000 pounds
Diet: Plants
Fossils found: North America

Even the hungriest meat eater of the Mesozoic would find *Ankylosaurus* hard to swallow. As long as it stayed flat against the ground, and didn't let a hunter get to its soft underbelly, it was safe from predators. That's because the top of *Ankylosaurus* was covered in hard, bony plates. At 8 feet wide and 6 feet tall, *Ankylosaurus* was as big as a small truck.

Ankylosaurus had a bony knob at the end of its tail that it swung like a club.

The top of *Ankylosaurus*'s body was covered in hard, bony plates that protected it against predators—especially *Tyrannosaurus rex*.

Ankylosaurus's beak and small teeth were perfect for eating plants.

Short, stout legs put *Ankylosaurus* low to the ground, allowing it to graze on plants.

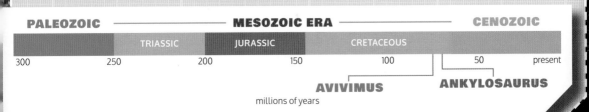

PALEOZOIC		MESOZOIC ERA			CENOZOIC	
		TRIASSIC	JURASSIC	CRETACEOUS		
300	250	200	150	100	50	present

AVIVIMUS

ANKYLOSAURUS

millions of years

CRETACEOUS DINOSAURS

CORYTHOSAURUS

Corythosaurus means "Corinthian helmet lizard." It's thought that Corythosaurus probably used the large crest on its head like a one-note musical instrument.

Corythosaurus had a crest on its head that looked similar to helmets worn by ancient Greeks. It was made from bony material, and helped Corythosaurus make loud trumpeting noises.

A flattened beak contained sharp teeth for chewing plants.

Corythosaurus

Name meaning:
Corinthian helmet lizard
Size: 33 feet long; 8,000 pounds
Diet: Plants
Fossils found: North America

Triceratops

Name meaning: Three-horned face
Size: 30 feet long; 12,000 pounds
Diet: Plants
Fossils found: North America

TRICERATOPS

Meat-eating dinosaurs were fearsome killers, so plant-eating dinosaurs needed a way to protect themselves. Some, like *Triceratops*, developed tough skin and horns for protection. *Triceratops* had three sharp horns on its head to defend itself, and a big frill on its neck. A bony plate not only made *Triceratops* look bigger than it really was, but may also have prevented attackers from reaching behind its head to get at its body.

Young *Triceratops* had frills but they grew larger in adults. Scientists believe that they were useful in attracting mates.

Triceratops's sharp teeth were continuously shed and replaced throughout its life.

A powerful beak helped *Triceratops* crush through tough plants.

Triceratops had short, strong legs with hoof-like claws. Although it had short legs and a bulky body, *Triceratops* could run up to 20 miles per hour.

PALEOZOIC		MESOZOIC ERA			CENOZOIC
	TRIASSIC	JURASSIC	CRETACEOUS		
300	250	200	150	100	50	present

CORYTHOSAURUS   TRICERATOPS

millions of years

CRETACEOUS DINOSAURS

PACHYCEPHALOSAURUS

Pachycephalosaurus is the largest known bone—headed dinosaur. *Pachycephalosaurus* had a skull that was 20 times thicker than other dinosaurs. Scientists believe they had such thick skulls because they may have used their heads for defense or for attack.

Pachycephalosaurus

Name meaning: Thick-headed lizard

Size: 15 feet long; 1,000 pounds

Diet: Plants

Fossils found: North America

The dome of Pachycephalosaurus's head was surrounded by a crown of spikes that are thought to be used for defense.

Pachycephalosaurus walked on its strong hind legs.

Its snout was covered in small spikes and horns.

Pachycephalosaurus's back legs each contained four toes.

TYRANNOSAURUS REX

The most infamous of all the dinosaurs, the meat-eating *T.rex* was a fierce hunter with lots of sharp teeth and a powerful bite. *T.rex*'s arms were unusually small and short, but were surprisingly strong. Recent discoveries suggest that the *T.rex* may have been partially covered in feathers!

Its sharp teeth, up to 12 inches long, were ridged to tear though meat.

A long, thick tail balanced *T.rex*'s enormous body and helped it move quickly.

Tyrannosaurus rex

Name meaning: Tyrant lizard king
Size: 40 feet long; 15,000 pounds
Diet: Large and small animals
Fossils found: Western United States and Canada

PALEOZOIC	MESOZOIC ERA			CENOZOIC
	TRIASSIC	JURASSIC	CRETACEOUS	
300	250	200	150	100	50	present

PACHYCEPHALOSAURUS   T.REX

millions of years

39

DINOSAUR EXTINCTION

Dinosaurs roamed Earth for 165 million years—that's much longer than the 200,000 years that humans have existed. Scientists are constantly uncovering new clues and learning more about the complexity of dinosaurs. And they are still continuing to search for answers to the cause of the dinosaurs' extinction.

There are many theories that try to explain how dinosaurs disappeared. Although these theories differ, they all agree on one thing: climate change. Toward the end of the Cretaceous period, the climate started to cool.

THEORY 1

One theory involves the increase of volcanic activity at the time. The volcanoes likely released sulphur and carbon dioxide into the air, which resulted in global warming. Eventually, the pollutants would have settled back to earth and the temperature would have risen abruptly. This quick change in the climate would have been too much for some species to handle. If this theory caused the extinction of the dinosaurs, it wouldn't have happened quickly. The fossil records show that extinction and recovery happened over 500,000 years.

The dinosaurs weren't the only casualties of this mass extinction. Flying reptiles like pterosaurs, some ocean life, and many insects and plant species were also wiped out.

PALEOZOIC		MESOZOIC ERA		CENOZOIC
	TRIASSIC	JURASSIC	CRETACEOUS	
300	250	200	150	100	50	present

millions of years

EXTINCTION

DINOSAUR EXTINCTION

THEORY 2

Due to evidence of an impact site in Central America, scientists believe that an asteroid smashed into Earth around the time the dinosaurs began to go extinct. This would have caused dust to rise into the air and block out the Sun, which may have cooled the climate. Others believe that many asteroid impacts in a very short amount of time caused the dinosaurs' extinction.

FACT

Many scientists point to the 110-mile-wide Chicxulub crater in Mexico as the point of asteroid impact that caused the mass extinction 66 million years ago.

THEORY 3

The third theory combines theories one and two. A layer of rock from 66 million years ago is found all around the world and contains a metal called iridium. There are two places where this metal is found. The first is the Earth's core. Magma, the molten rock that spews out of volcanoes, comes out of Earth's core and contains iridium. The second place iridium is found is in meteorites.

FOSSILS

Today, no living dinosaurs walk the planet, except for birds, descendants of dinosaurs. Everything we know about dinosaurs we've learned by studying their fossils. Fossils are the remains of animals preserved in the earth. If a living thing dies and happens to be buried in a way that keeps air, scavengers, and bacteria from getting to it, it can become a fossil.

HOW FOSSILS ARE FORMED

To become a fossil, dinosaurs needed to be covered by sand, mud, or water right after they died. If it gets exposed to the air or elements, it will decompose before it can fossilize. As years go by, the dead dinosaur gets buried deeper and deeper under rocky layers of sediment. Minerals from the sediment seep into and replace the dinosaur's bones as the ground around the dinosaur hardens.

Eventually, the minerals and the bones merge together and a rocky copy of the dinosaur is made. As the ground shifts, the fossil gets pushed to the surface to be discovered. Scientists can date a fossil by examining the rock and other fossils that surround it or by measuring its radioactive decay in Uranium or Zircon in the rocks that contain the fossils.

FOSSILS

Paleontologists can examine fossilized dinosaur teeth to determine if the dinosaur was a plant-eater or meat-eater. Leaf-shaped teeth mean that the dinosaur most likely ate plants that had to be ground up. Sharp teeth mean that the dinosaur most likely ate meat and needed sharp teeth to tear meat from the bone.

You don't have to be a paleontologist to find a fossil. Everyday people, even kids, find most fossils! Only about one out of five fossils is actually discovered by a scientist. Scientists a hundred years ago only used shovels, chisels, and brushes to uncover fossils. Today, new technology allows scientists to discover fossils faster than ever.

WHAT BECOMES A FOSSIL?

Bones aren't the only part of an animal that can be fossilized. Footprints, feces, eggs, and feathers can be fossilized too.

Fossilized dinosaur dung is called coprolite. Coprolites can tell paleontologists what foods the dinosaur ate.

Some of the most important fossils scientists find are dinosaur tracks. Fossilized tracks illustrate how dinosaurs moved and whether or not they traveled in groups.

Even when scientists find a fossil, much of what they hypothesize comes from educated guesses and scientific study. That's because what's often found is just a small part of the creature. To determine what type of animal it came from, scientists consider where the fossils were discovered. Then they put the information together to come up with a good description of the animal. Often, it's like putting together a puzzle with missing pieces.

FOSSIL AND DINOSAUR DISCOVERIES

Although dinosaurs died millions of years ago, their fossilized bones remained intact under the earth and weren't discovered until hundreds of years ago. When looking at a timeline of when dinosaurs lived and when they were finally uncovered, dinosaurs are a recent discovery.

Did you know?
Fossil is from a Latin word meaning "dug up."

HISTORY OF PALEONTOLOGY

Prior to the 1800s, dinosaur bones were discovered, but were believed to belong to extinct animals, similar to those that are found on Earth today. Bones were uncovered all over the world and were interpreted differently depending on the culture. The ancient Chinese thought that dinosaur fossils were from magical dragons. In North America, the Sioux Native Americans believed that dinosaur bones belonged to giant serpents that burrowed deep underground.

Gideon Mantell: Dinosaurs in the United Kingdom

Gideon Mantell was a British physician, geologist, and paleontologist. He and his wife, Mary Ann Mantell, enjoyed going on digs in hope of discovering prehistoric creatures. In the 1820s, Gideon and Mary Ann made the first major fossil discoveries. In 1822, they unearthed teeth from the Mesozoic era. At first, other scientists dismissed them as rhinoceros teeth, but later Gideon found that they were from an ancient reptile he called "*Iguanodon*." Gideon played a vital role in paleontology and found four out of the five dinosaurs discovered at the time.

Portion of the Jaw of the Iguanodon, four times magnified.

19TH CENTURY		20TH CENTURY		21ST C
1800 1810 1820 1830 1840 1850 1860 1870 1880 1890	1900 1910 1920 1930 1940 1950 1960 1970 1980 1990	2000 2010 2020		

GIDEON MANTELL

THE BIRTH OF DINOSAURS

In 1842, Sir Richard Owen, one of the most important people in British paleontology, gave ancient reptiles the name "Dinosauria" meaning "Fearfully Great Reptiles." A British anatomist and paleontologist, Owen examined reptile-like fossils discovered in southern England by paleontologists such as Gideon Mantell. By studying these fossils, Owen concluded that the bones weren't from lizards, but part of a group he called dinosaurs. In addition to establishing London's Natural History Museum in 1881, Sir Richard Owen set the stage for placing the new discovery of ancient reptiles into their own distinct group.

Dinosaurs in the American West

Ferdinand Vandeveer Hayden was an American geologist who explored the Great Plains and Rocky Mountain regions of North America. Sponsored by the American Fur Company, Hayden explored and mapped the region around the Missouri River. In 1854, near the Missouri River, Hayden unearthed unusual teeth. He sent them to paleontologist Joseph Leidy who confirmed that they belonged to dinosaurs—some of the earliest dinosaurs discovered in the American west.

Hayden and his artist, Walter Paris

	19TH CENTURY	20TH CENTURY	21ST C

1800 1810 1820 1830 1840 1850 1860 1870 1880 1890 1900 1910 1920 1930 1940 1950 1960 1970 1980 1990 2000 2010 2020

SIR RICHARD OWEN   **FERDINAND VANDEVEER HAYDEN**

DINOSAUR IN NEW JERSEY

In 1858, William Parker Foulke, a geologist, discovered a partial skeleton of a dinosaur in Haddonfield, New Jersey. Not only was it the most complete skeleton discovered to date in the United States, but also contained enough bones to reconstruct its anatomy. The bones were shown to Joseph Leidy who called the dinosaur "*Hadrosaurus*." *Hadrosaurus* was a duck-billed herbivore that lived 80 million years ago. This monumental discovery not only influenced the field of paleontology, but was a major moment in New Jersey's history.

FACT
Hadrosaurus became the official state dinosaur of New Jersey in 1991!

THE DINOSAUR WARS (1877-1892)

For almost 30 years, two paleontologists, Othniel Charles Marsh and Edward Drinker Cope, headed to the American West to uncover prehistoric fossils. Whether fueled by their competitiveness or their passion for paleontology, Marsh and Cope discovered over 100 new species. Both men sought distinction in their field, and often sent their crews to spy on each other, or sometimes, steal each other's fossils.

By 1877, in Colorado and Wyoming, Marsh and Cope started uncovering the largest dinosaur fossils discovered at the time—those of *Stegosaurus* and *Allosaurus*.

Cartoon of Othniel Charles Marsh

Edward Drinker Cope

Othniel Charles Marsh

19TH CENTURY	20TH CENTURY	21ST C

| 1800 | 1810 | 1820 | 1830 | 1840 | 1850 | 1860 | 1870 | 1880 | 1890 | 1900 | 1910 | 1920 | 1930 | 1940 | 1950 | 1960 | 1970 | 1980 | 1990 | 2000 | 2010 | 2020 |

HADROSAURUS DISCOVERED

THE DINOSAUR WARS

GOBI DESERT DISCOVERIES

Roy Chapman Andrews was an American naturalist believed to be the inspiration for Hollywood's Indiana Jones. From 1922—1930, Andrews was sent on expeditions to the Gobi Desert, located in Asia from southern Mongolia to northwestern China.

Utilizing the new invention of automobiles with the traditional mode of transportation, camels, Andrews explored the Gobi Desert; little did he know that he'd make one of the most important discoveries in paleontology. Andrews discovered the first nest of dinosaur eggs that proved that dinosaurs laid eggs and hatched from them. In addition, Andrews discovered new species, including *Velociraptor*, as well as mammals that coexisted with the dinosaurs.

SUE THE *T.REX*

The most famous American dinosaur that was discovered in the last 50 years is on display at the Field Museum in Chicago, Illinois. Its name is Sue (although scientists are unsure if it's a female or male) and it's the largest, best-preserved *Tyrannosaurus rex* ever found. The dinosaur is 42 feet long and 13 feet tall at the hip.

Sue was discovered on August 12, 1990, on the Cheyenne River Sioux Indian Reservation in South Dakota. Paleontologist Sue Hendrickson, whom the dinosaur was named after, uncovered her. It took a crew of six people 17 days to unearth the giant *T.rex*!

Sue the *T.rex*

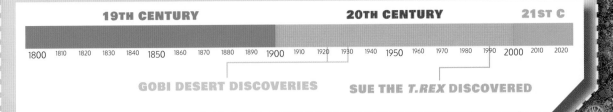

19TH CENTURY								20TH CENTURY								21ST C	
1800	1810	1820	1830	1840	1850	1860	1870	1880	1890	1900	1910	1920	1930	1940	1950	1960	1970	1980	1990	2000	2010	2020

GOBI DESERT DISCOVERIES   SUE THE *T.REX* DISCOVERED

DISCOVERY BY A 16-YEAR-OLD

Although professional paleontologists have made major dinosaur discoveries, there have been other instances where fossils have been uncovered by people who weren't intentionally looking for them. In 1999, 16-year-old Tyler Lyson discovered an impressive fossil on his uncle's farm in North Dakota. Lyson discovered a *Hadrosaur*, a duck-billed dinosaur, that was found nearly complete, and still had skin, bones, and tendons. The fossil Lyson found, named "Dakota," was 25 feet long and died 76 million years ago. Lyson's discovery influenced him to continue studying and digging up dinosaurs—Lyson later received his PhD in paleontology and studied at the Smithsonian Institution as a post-doctoral fellow.

Dakota's skin impression

SOPHIE THE STEGOSAURUS

Sophie the Stegosaurus

An almost-complete *Stegosaurus* was discovered in 2003 at Red Canyon Ranch in Wyoming. It was uncovered by paleontologist Bob Simon.

The 150–million–year–old dinosaur took three weeks to remove from the earth. Like Sue the *T. rex*, it is unknown whether Sophie was male or female, but scientists do know that it was young when it died.

19TH CENTURY										20TH CENTURY										21ST C
1800	1810	1820	1830	1840	1850	1860	1870	1880	1890	1900	1910	1920	1930	1940	1950	1960	1970	1980	1990	2000	2010	2020

"DAKOTA" DISCOVERED   "SOPHIE" DISCOVERED

BIRDS: MODERN-DAY DINOSAURS

Most scientists think modern birds are the last living relatives of the giant dinosaurs of the Mesozoic. In fact, we know that *Tyrannosaurus rex*, one of the biggest, scariest beasts that ever walked the earth, is more closely related to birds than it is to any other animal alive today.

Birds descended from a group of dinosaurs called theropods, two-legged dinosaurs. *Velociraptor* was a member of this group. Feathers were once believed to have been a unique feature of birds. However, in the 1990s dinosaur fossils from China were found with feathers! Feathers on both dinosaurs and birds were an even more important connection between the two.

Next time you look up at the sky and see birds soaring above, think about how they came from ancestors who lived in a world much different than ours today. Their ancestors were fantastic creatures that were fierce and ferocious, big and small. Perhaps next time you see a bird, it will inspire you to explore the wonderful world of dinosaurs!

PALEOZOIC		MESOZOIC ERA		CENOZOIC
	TRIASSIC	JURASSIC	CRETACEOUS	
300	250	200	150	100	50	present

BIRDS

DINOSAUR FAMILY GROUPS

Orthinopod

Iguanodon

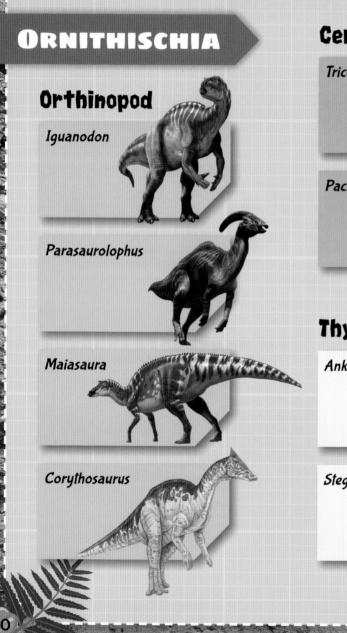

Parasaurolophus

Maiasaura

Corythosaurus

Cerapoda

Triceratops

Pachycephalosaurus

Thyreophora

Ankylosaurus

Stegosaurus

SAURICHIA

Theropods

Eoraptor

Spinosaurus

Coelophysis

Velociraptor

Allosaurus

Tyrannosaurus Rex

Archaeopteryx

Avivimus

Utahraptor

Sauropod

Plateosaurus

Diplodocus

Apatosaurus

Brachiosaurus

Amargasaurus

Argentinosaurus

GLOSSARY

Camouflage: animal coloring and texture that enables it to blend in with its surroundings

Crest: growth on an animal's head

Dinosaur: the main group of the archosaur reptiles that dominated the land during the Mesozoic er

Extinction: no longer living

Fossil: body part, footprint, or other remains of a dead plant or animal that has turned to stone. Evidence of life from the geologic past

Coprolite: fossilized dinosaur dung

Geologist: scientist who studies the earth and its processes

Prehistoric: term used to describe the time before people began recording history

Herbivore: animal that only eats plants

Prey: animals that are hunted by other animals for food

Protofeather: primitive feather found in some fossils

Paleontologist: scientist who studies fossils

Pangaea: the supercontinent made up of all the landmasses on Earth that began breaking up during the end of the Triassic period

Vertebrae: bones that make up the spine

T. REX MODEL INSTRUCTIONS

1

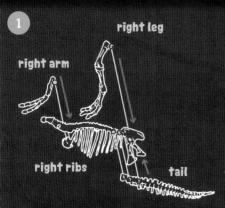

right leg

right arm

right ribs

tail

Connect the T. rex's right arm and right leg to the right ribs of the T. rex's body. Next, snap the tail onto the end. Set it aside.

2

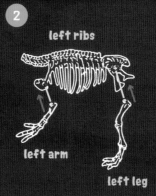

left ribs

left arm

left leg

Now, attach the T. rex's left arm and left leg to the left ribs of the T. rex's body. Set it aside.

3

right skull

jaw

left skull

Connect the T. rex's jaw to the skull, then press the halves together and connect them to the spine.

4

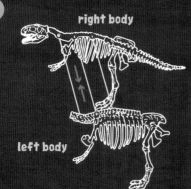

right body

left body

Line up the two halves of the body and press to connect them together.

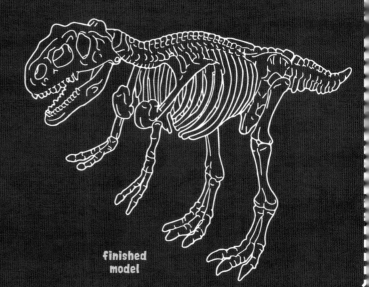

finished model